Glasgow
Pocket Guide

Kenneth Walton

Colin Baxter Photography Limited, Grantown-on-Spey, Scotland

First published in Great Britain in 1999 by
Colin Baxter Photography Ltd, Grantown-on-Spey, Moray PH26 3NA, Scotland

Front Cover Photographs (clockwise):
Glasgow Art Gallery and Museum / The River Clyde / Tenements, Great Western Road /
(inset) Charles Rennie Mackintosh: bookcase detail (Glasgow School of Art)
Back Cover Photograph: Glasgow's coat of arms on a lamppost, Cathedral Square
Page 2 Photograph: Doorway, West End
Page 70 Photograph: Glasgow Art Gallery and Museum, Kelvingrove

A CIP record for this book is available from the British Library

ISBN 1 900455 56 0

Printed in Hong Kong

Glasgow
Pocket Guide

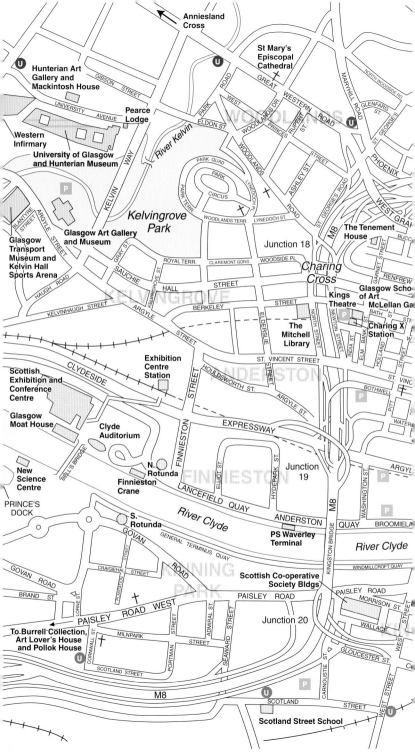

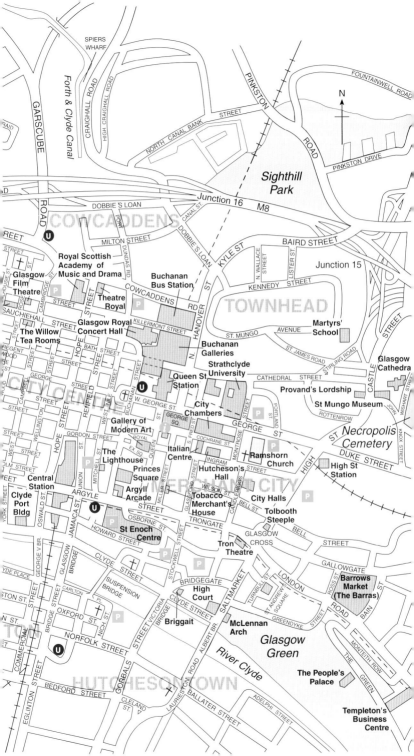

INTRODUCTION

A simple rhyme refers to emblems pictured on Glasgow's coat of arms:

> *Here's the Bird that never flew, Here's the Tree that never grew*
> *Here's the Bell that never rang, Here's the Fish that never swam.*

Of these, the Tree symbolises the hazel branch which the young Saint Mungo miraculously set alight when the holy fire of the monastery was mischievously extinguished by the other boys; the Bird is the robin he brought back to life after St Serf's disciples had killed it and blamed Mungo; the Fish refers to the story of Queen Langeoreth whose husband, King Rydderach Hael, suspecting her of infidelity, challenged her to produce the golden wedding ring he believed she had given to a young knight. The queen, instructed by Mungo to take a salmon from the river, was amazed, and presumably relieved, to discover the missing gold ring inside the salmon's mouth.

These legendary episodes from the life of Glasgow's patron saint, St Mungo, are all potent symbols of rebirth, a quality which is a recurring theme in Glasgow's long and fascinating history.

This *Pocket Guide* relates something of that history, and introduces the reader to the obvious, and not so obvious, sights around the city, each of which has its own place and significance in the story of this great city.

Glasgow – A Great European City of Culture

Today, Glasgow is one of the UK's most visited cities. The city that hosted the highly popular Glasgow Garden Festival in 1988, was European City of Culture in 1990, and mounted the spectacular Glasgow Festival of Visual Arts in 1996, welcomes tourists from all over the world each year who are drawn by its wealth of cultural attractions and activities.

City of History

Around Glasgow, ancient buildings and historical streets and monuments relate a fascinating and influential past.

City of Architecture

Glasgow's architecture is among the finest in Europe and Glasgow was designated UK City of Architecture and Design in 1999. Its streets are lined with row upon row of beautifully preserved Victorian buildings.

City of Museums and Galleries
Glasgow has over twenty wonderful museums and galleries, each with its own individual collection and events programme, and most with free admission.

City of Arts and Entertainment
The city that hosted the Great Exhibitions of 1888 and 1901, and was designated European City of Culture 1990, has a full and exciting range of entertainment venues and activities.

City of Parks and Gardens
The name Glasgow means 'dear green place', recognising the fact that Glasgow has more parks and open spaces than any other city its size. Many of them contain some of the city's main galleries and attractions, facilities for recreational activities, and some fine examples of Victorian sculpture.

City of Sport
Sport is an integral part of Glasgow's culture, reflected in the city's designation as a UK National City of Sport 1996-99. Scotland's most famous football teams, Glasgow Rangers and Celtic, are an integral part of Glasgow's culture.

City of Retail and Shopping
Glasgow has the UK's largest retail sector outwith London. Residents and visitors from around the UK and overseas are drawn to the city's expanding shopping outlets.

City of Learning
Since the city's first university was established in 1451, Glasgow has been hailed as a powerful seat of learning. Lord Kelvin (William Thomson), Adam Smith and James Watt are just some of history's great thinkers associated with the city's academic past.

The Friendly City
Glasgow has a reputation for being the friendliest city in the world. Its people are welcoming, cheery and, above all, think nothing of going out of their way to help visitors. No one is a stranger in Glasgow.

THE STORY OF GLASGOW

Early Settlements

Glasgow, Scotland's largest city, has a history stretching back to earliest times.

Along the banks of the River Clyde, the remnants of Stone Age canoes found over the years are evidence of early fishing communities in the area that was to become, by the 19th century, Scotland's busiest and wealthiest port.

Celtic druids were among the first identifiable tribes to have lived in the area. They probably traded with the Romans who, around AD 80, would have had a trading post in Cathures, the earlier name for Glasgow.

Beyond AD 380, when the great Christian missionary St Ninian passed through Cathures and consecrated a burial ground, little is known until the arrival of St Kentigern in the 6th century.

St Mungo and the Birth of a City

St Kentigern settled in Glasgow (or *Glas cu*, meaning 'dear green place') in AD 543 following exile from Culross, where his monastic brothers had grown jealous of his miraculous powers.

In Glasgow, he established his Christian church on the banks of the Molendinar river. Such was his popularity, the people named him Mungo, meaning 'dear one', the name by which today's great cathedral is known. When he died, he was buried in Glasgow within his own church.

Between St Mungo's death and Glasgow's establishment as an Episcopal See in 1115, little is known of the city's history. But with its newly acquired religious authority, and the wealth of lands now held south of the River Forth under the new bishopric, Glasgow was by 1172 a significant and powerful city. Its new stone cathedral, consecrated in 1136, stood proud and protective high above the lively salmon and herring fishing village on the Clyde.

◀ *Glasgow's High Street marks the ancient downhill route from St Mungo's Cathedral Church to Glasgow Cross. At its southern end, the towering 17th-century Tolbooth Steeple dominates the approach to the Cross and presents today's traffic with a major obstacle. Surrounded nowadays by a mixture of later architectural styles it is, along with the nearby Tron Steeple, one of the very few remaining symbols of the area's former significance.*

While Glasgow was powerful in terms of its religious status, it was not in terms of trade. William the Lion's charter in 1180, which made Glasgow a burgh, opened the doors to commerce and Glasgow's future as a city built on its ability to do business around the world.

And yet Glasgow was not a Royal Burgh, a factor which placed limitations on its trading position. That was to change in 1450 when James II issued a charter to the bishop 'erecting all his patrimony into a regality' – a Royal Burgh in all but name.

Thus began a 50-year period which was to see the city's status enhanced considerably, firstly with the establishment of the University of Glasgow in 1451, and then with its elevation to an archbishopric in 1492.

Glasgow was, by the end of the 15th century, a powerful academic and ecclesiastical centre, rivalled only by St Andrews in the east.

The Rise of the Merchant Trader

In 1560, following the Reformation, the last Roman Catholic archbishop, James Beaton, fled to Paris, along with many of the cathedral's records and treasured relics. Unlike many of Scotland's cathedrals, Glasgow Cathedral had survived this religious onslaught, despite the wish of the principal of the university, Andrew Melville, to have it pulled down and new churches built in its place. The guilds protested, Melville capitulated, and Glasgow possesses one of the few complete examples in Scotland of pre-Reformation cathedral churches.

Beaton's exile marked the move towards greater civic power, and the emerging influence of the city's merchants and craftsmen.

Trade was undoubtedly booming by the time Oliver Cromwell visited Glasgow in 1650. His agent, Thomas Tucker, recognised the city's great potential, were it not 'checqed and kept under by the shallowness of the river.'

▶ *Glasgow's oldest residential house, the 15th-century Provand's Lordship, occupies a prominent position at the foot of Castle Street facing Cathedral Square. It is believed to have been the residence of one of the many Canons of the Cathedral – the Lord of the Prebend of Barlanark – whose lands were known as the Lordship of Provand.*

The 18th Century and New Opportunities

When Scotland eventually turned to the Atlantic for trade opportunities, Glasgow came into its own. It was ideally placed, on the west coast. A dynamic business community seized the opportunity.

By the early 1700s, substantial quantities of tobacco were being shipped in from American tobacco states. Glasgow's merchants, in turn, had contracts to supply Europe. By 1730, trade with America was fully established. Glasgow's Tobacco Lords had cornered the market, becoming Glasgow's and Scotland's first millionaires.

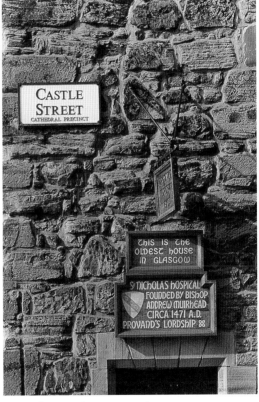

Glasgow took more than half of the American tobacco crop. One merchant, John Glassford, who owned 25 ships, re-exported 80% of his imports to the continent, grossing £500,000 a year.

Daniel Defoe, sent to Glasgow as a government agent to promote the Union with England, wrote in 1724 about its profitable effect on Glasgow: 'The Union has indeed answered its end to them more than to any other part of the Kingdom... they now send near fifty ships every year to Virginia.'

Such wealth began to have an impact on Glasgow's geography. A New Town was beginning to emerge as the thriving merchant community began to move west from Saltmarket and Bridgegate to the area we now know as the Merchant City. Grand mansions were built, as were banks, warehouses and other public buildings.

The American Revolution dealt a vicious blow in 1775. Those who had invested solely in the tobacco

trade suffered literally overnight. However, many merchants had diversified into trade with the West Indies, importing sugar and rum. By the end of the 18th century Glasgow had become Britain's biggest importer of sugar.

The age-old problem of making the river navigable had now been overcome. In 1770, John Golborne, a civil engineer from Chester, had devised a means of flushing the silt layers naturally out from the bed of the shallow Clyde by erecting a series of jetties along its banks. By 1772 large vessels were able to sail up the river into the city for the first time.

Second City of the Empire

As the 19th century dawned, and the Industrial Revolution took hold, Glasgow's new industrialists were expanding their businesses, particularly in cotton and textiles, chemicals, glass, paper and soap manufacturing. The population was increasing rapidly as immigrants from the Highlands in the 1820s, and from Ireland in the 1840s, provided the unskilled labour required.

The cotton industry, at its height, employed almost a third of Glasgow's workforce, but like the tobacco industry, it was to be badly affected by external factors – the American Civil War of 1861, and nearer to home, tough competition from cities like Manchester.

Ever resourceful, the city turned to industries like shipbuilding, locomotive construction and other heavy engineering which could thrive on nearby supplies of coal and iron ore.

Between 1870 and 1914, Glasgow ranked as one of the richest and finest cities in Europe. It was hailed as a model of organised industrial society, governed by a benevolent council. Great public buildings, museums, galleries and libraries, were erected, Glasgow had more parks and open spaces than any other European city its size, and it had a regulated telephone system, as well as water and gas supplies.

The two Great Exhibitions of 1881 and 1901, both in Kelvingrove Park, displayed Glasgow's pride in its achievements. Glasgow was, without a doubt, the 'Second City of the Empire.'

Industrial Decline

The story of 20th-century Glasgow, at least after the First World War, is in stark contrast to the previous century, with industrial decline of enormous proportions.

Rearmament of the navy in the post-war 1930s, and once again the need for the country to replace vessels after the Second World War, stalled the

◄ 19th-century Glasgow architecture at its most flamboyant. Charing Cross Mansions form a bold and gracious curve at the westernmost end of the city centre on Sauchiehall Street. The attic windows and centre-piece clock offer more than a hint of French influence, a style echoed in nearby Park Circus.

process to some extent. The launch of the great Cunard liners, the *Queen Mary* and *Queen Elizabeth* in the 1930s, and the Empire Exhibition of 1938, remained proud moments for Glasgow. 'Clyde-built' still meant quality.

By the 1950s, however, there was little demand for merchant or navy ships. The heavy industries which had brought the city unparalleled wealth and fame, could no longer compete with the cheaper labour costs of their emerging overseas competitors and, for the shipbuilders, the modern world of air travel.

Cultural Renaissance

What Glasgow did have, was the tangible legacy left by its wealthy and munificent merchant traders and industrial barons, a great architectural and cultural heritage.

Charles Rennie Mackintosh's Willow Tea Rooms. Even today his unique style of bright internal furnishings remains undated and genuinely novel.

As the cleaning-up process of the 1970s and 1980s proved, the gleaming gold and red sandstone, hidden behind decades of industrial soot and grime, revealed the finest examples of Victorian architecture anywhere in the world. Here was a backdrop against which to position Glasgow as a great European city of culture.

The unique art nouveau designs of Charles Rennie Mackintosh, never truly appreciated in their time, were now of considerable interest in and around the city; there were over twenty museums and galleries housing their own wonderful, eclectic collections; Glasgow was the home to Scottish Opera and Scottish Ballet, two national symphony orchestras, the Theatre Royal, the Royal Scottish Academy of Music and Drama; the city had a varied range of cultural activities which could play a part in what was to prove both an economic and cultural renaissance.

Glasgow now attracts tourists from all over the world who appreciate Daniel Defoe's description

of Glasgow as being 'one of the cleanliest, most beautiful and best built cities in Great Britain.'

The city has established a new economic base centred on the service sector, and has risen from a period of industrial decline to mount a highly successful Garden Festival in 1988, a year of international arts festivities in 1990 to celebrate its reign as European City of Culture, and a Festival of Visual Arts in 1996 which saw the opening of the new Gallery of Modern Art, and a major retrospective exhibition of the life of Charles Rennie Mackintosh.

To have finished the millennium as UK City of Architecture and Design 1999 seems entirely appropriate.

The site of Glasgow's 1988 National Garden Festival on reclaimed land on the south bank of the River Clyde is set to become the location of a new multi-million pound Science Centre.

HIGH STREET & THE OLD TOWN

Today's visitor to Glasgow, standing in the flow line of the Molendinar Burn, as St Mungo might have done in the 6th century, gazing up at the city's magnificent 13th-century Cathedral, will not get his feet wet. The shallow, winding river, so closely associated with the founding saint, and above which he built his original timber and wattle church, was covered over during the 18th century to conceal what had become a filthy sewer, and today it runs under concrete and stone for all of its journey to the River Clyde.

Wishart Street follows the line of the river, from which rises dramatically the Necropolis burial ground to the east and the Cathedral to the west. From under the stark Roman arch of the **Bridge of Sighs** – the imposing edifice built by Glasgow's wealthy merchants to create a level walkway across the river from the Necropolis – the view of the Cathedral is stunning, revealing the ingenious two-storey double choir at the east end, built to accommodate the steep slope down to the river, and to incorporate St Mungo's tomb.

Glasgow Cathedral itself is a wonderful example of pre-Reformation Gothic architecture, modest in size, but remarkable in its unity of style and quirky idiosyncrasies. The lower Laigh Kirk, a labyrinth of vaults and columns under the main choir, operated as a separate church between the Reformation and the late 18th century, after which it was used as a burial ground.

In this dark and peaceful sub-chamber lies St Mungo's shrine, a series of small chapels and, protruding from the south at the spot reputedly where St Ninian consecrated his 5th-century cemetery, the surprisingly radiant white glow of the Blacader Isle. Built by Archbishop Blacader around the 15th or 16th century, its roof vaulting is impressively capped with medieval carved bosses.

▶ *Glasgow Cathedral marks the site where Glasgow's patron saint, Mungo, is buried. One of its most spectacular viewpoints is from the higher ground of the Necropolis. Note the consistency of architectural style throughout the 13th-century cathedral, and the ingenious two-storey choir at the east end.*

The main church is a triumph of simplicity and beauty, the narrow and lofty nave and choir belying the relatively modest proportions of the building. A striking 15th-century carved rood screen, supporting the 19th-century Willis organ, separates the nave from the choir. At the east end lies the exquisite Lady Chapel.

The **Necropolis**, the opulent burial ground set high above the Cathedral, was created by

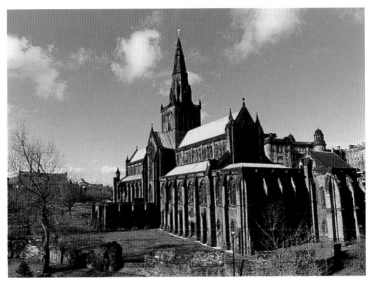

Glasgow's wealthy merchants in 1833. John Bryce's design for the former Fir Park is based on the famous Père Lachaise cemetery in Paris, and features myriad catacombs, vaults and mausoleums through which the great and the good of 19th-century Glasgow sought immortality. The most prominent edifice remains the towering monument to John Knox, created in 1825 prior to the area's use as a graveyard. Of curiosity value is the cenotaph to William Miller, author of the children's rhyme, *Wee Willie Winkie*.

The domed frontage of James Miller's **Glasgow Infirmary** rather dominates the re-landscaped paved avenue which leads to the west door of the

Cathedral from Castle Street. Its grim and bulky proportions were intended as a tribute to the similar, but more refined, design by Robert Adam which it replaced in 1914.

The newly created buildings opposite have been more sensitively conceived, in particular the mock baronial **St Mungo Museum of Religious Life and Art**. Opened in 1992, the museum has an illuminating presentation of artefacts relating

to the world's six major religions, particularly those which have helped shape modern-day Glasgow. Among the exhibits is probably Glasgow's most famous painting (slashed more than once in its old Kelvingrove Art Gallery setting by religious vandals), the stunning and controversial *Christ of St John on the Cross* by Salvador Dali. From the second-floor landing, the prominent view of John Knox's statue high on the Necropolis seems delightfully provocative. The delicate Zen Garden is a tranquil oasis within Cathedral Square.

Of the many residential buildings that once surrounded the Cathedral precincts, only the **Provand's Lordship** on Castle Street remains, the oldest house in Glasgow, dating from 1471. During a visit there in 1567, Mary Queen of Scots is said to have planned the murder of Darnley. The house contains 16th-century furnishings and some fine stained glass, and an art gallery on the top floor.

On the south gable wall is the well-worn coat of arms of Andrew Muirhead, one of Glasgow's medieval bishops; and to the west, the newly created **St Nicholas Gardens**, a walled 'Physic Garden' named after the original 15th-century St Nicholas Hospital which Muirhead founded.

Just visible at the top of Castle Street is one of several wonderful buildings by the celebrated Glasgow architect Charles Rennie Mackintosh, the red sandstone **Martyrs' School**.

Cathedral Square stands surrounded by a curious, but interesting collection of buildings. Most prominent is the substantial Early English Gothic **Barony Church**, now Strathclyde University's graduation hall, completed in 1890 by Sir J J Burnet and John A Campbell to replace the original Barony Church which lay on the other side of the Square, and which was by all accounts a hideous building, described by Queen Victoria's chaplain as 'the ugliest Kirk in all Europe.'

John Honeyman's 1878 **Barony North Church** (now Glasgow Evangelical Church) strikes a graceful presence opposite, with its slender Italianate columns topped by statues, elegant belfry and gleaming white sandstone. The adjacent **Cathedral House Hotel**, in rugged baronial style, was originally a halfway house for discharged female prisoners.

The 1960s **Ladywell** housing development, reasonable for its time, lines the bottom edge of the Square, where once Duke Street Prison was.

Among the statues which adorn the Cathedral precincts are John Mossman's 1879 bronze statue of David Livingstone, moved from George Square in 1959, and that of King William III. This bronze statue was originally sited opposite the old Tontine

◄ *Recent years have seen the re-landscaping of Cathedral Square and the creation of a grand paved avenue leading up to the Cathedral gates from Castle Street. The area features statues by Mossman of such eminent Scots as the missionary David Livingstone and the Revd Dr Norman Macleod, chaplain to Queen Victoria and minister of the old Barony Church. The new St Mungo Museum of Religious Life and Art sits opposite the dominant frontage of the Royal Infirmary.*

Building at Glasgow Cross; close inspection reveals that the tail of the King's horse is attached with a ball and socket joint which lets it sway in the wind.

The crossing of High Street at the Barony Church represents Glasgow's original Market Cross, known as the Bell o' the Brae, marking the intersection with **Rottenrow** and the **Drygate**. The latter has been obliterated by the Ladywell houses, and Rottenrow is now mostly a private thoroughfare forming part of Strathclyde University's rapidly expanding student campus. Given that a house on Rottenrow provided one of the original homes for the medieval Glasgow University, the current development does not seem so inappropriate.

The **Bell o' the Brae** was, reputedly, the scene of Glasgow's first battle when, around 1300, William Wallace defeated an English garrison based in the Bishop's Castle.

In Wallace's time, the descent down **High Street** was precariously steep. But regular excavations over the centuries have levelled it out, and today's gentle slope is pleasantly complemented by the sweep of red sandstone tenements which date from 1901.

The junction with **Duke Street** and **George Street** reveals an impressive view: to the east along Duke Street (Britain's longest urban street), where the **Great Eastern Hotel** (a hostel, formerly **Alexander's Cotton Mill**), John Burnet's **Ladywell School** (funded by the same James Alexander), and the Greek-columned **Kirkhaven** (originally the 1851 Sydney Place Presbyterian Church) are all worth a look. Then glance westwards into the distance, to **St George's Tron Church**.

The remaining few hundred yards of High Street bear little resemblance to the thriving university area it once was. College Lands, latterly a busy railway goods depot, lies mainly derelict,

► *The dramatic downward sweep of Burnet & Boston's crow-stepped tenement buildings follows the gentle curve of High Street as it proceeds from Cathedral Square to its junction with Duke Street and the area once occupied by the original Glasgow University buildings. The journey down High Street was not always so smooth. A series of excavations over the years has gradually levelled out the once precariously steep descent.*

except for the Italian palazzo-style warehouses towards the bottom of the street, now converted to flats.

A few buildings on the west side deserve mention, and reflect the scattered remnants of bygone times which mark today's High Street. **Old College Bar**, set within a small cluster of older-looking buildings, claims to have been the oldest public house in Glasgow. A rather lean, striking red sand-

stone building stands incongruously nearby. Its fine Renaissance details and elegant cupola once housed the **British Linen Bank**, built in 1895.

At this point, the streets which branch off High Street provide a collection of concealed gems. The **Fire Station** on Ingram Street, now a restaurant, is a delightful curiosity. Built in 1900 to accommodate the original horse-drawn fenders, the narrow doors reflect this. If the interior Grecian marble walls seem a little ostentatious for such a utilitarian building, it was only because such superior building material was surplus to requirements at the nearby City Chambers.

Blackfriars Street possesses a little treasure

in **Babbity Bowster's** bar and bistro – the sole survivor of the original Stirling's Square, designed by James Adam in 1792, and recreated in its current form in 1986.

At the foot of High Street, the **Tolbooth**, an austere seven-storey tower with crown spire, dominates Glasgow Cross, mainly because its isolated

position in the middle of the road also presents something of a traffic hazard! Built in 1626, it formed the easternmost part of the building which housed Glasgow's first town hall and jail.

Up to the end of the 18th century, the Tolbooth was adorned with spikes on which were stuck the heads of those executed by the authorities. Its name derives from the fact that it housed the city's official weighing machine.

The **Mercat Cross** (a 1929 replica of the original, removed in 1659) dominates the east corner of Glasgow Cross, its octagonal plinth and unicorn-topped column set against the early 20th-century **Mercat Buildings**.

To the west runs **Trongate**, a street which enjoyed its heyday as Glasgow's 18th-century tobacco lords prospered. Then, the former Tontine Hotel and Coffee Room, accessed through the elegantly arcaded former Town Hall buildings, became prominent as an exclusive meeting place for the leading merchants of the day to exchange gossip and, no doubt, seal deals. Today's red sandstone office block replaced the original building after it burned down in 1911.

Of the street's earliest features, only the **Tron Steeple** (1636) remains, a part survivor of the original St Mary's Collegiate Church which was burned down by members of the notorious Hell Fire Club in 1793. James Adam's replacement church, set apart and behind the steeple, now operates as the **Tron Theatre**. Recent renovation of the Tron Theatre complex, in particular the addition of a new bar and restaurant, has much improved its facilities and appeal.

For the most part, however, all that remains of Glasgow's principal trading street are miscellaneous remnants. The Scottish baronial style **Tron House** at the corner of Albion Street was originally the headquarters of the ill-fated City of Glasgow Bank. Opposite, the frayed blue exterior of the old **Britannia Music Hall** (which still houses the shell of the original auditorium) provided the setting for Stan Laurel's stage debut.

The route east from Glasgow Cross along Gallowgate takes you to the famous **Barras** weekend street market – a Glasgow institution as famous for its colourful traders as for the exhaustive range of goods on offer. It sits behind the **Barrowland Ballroom**, for decades the city's prime entertainment venue hosting bandleaders from Joe Loss to Jack Hilton.

Saltmarket, immediately south of the Cross was, at various times, an area of respectable 18th-century dwellings for the wealthy merchants, and in the 19th century one of grim deprivation and ill repute. Nowadays, its broad line of clean tenements leads respectably to the impressive domed tower of the **Ship Bank Building** (1904) at the junction with Bridgegate.

Off to the left is **St Andrew's Square**, dominated by the bold baroque structure of **St Andrew's Church** (1739-59), hailed as one of Scotland's

◄ Up until the end of the 18th century, the heads of criminals executed by the authorities were impaled on spikes high up on the seven-storey Tolbooth Steeple. Built in 1626 as part of the larger Tolbooth building, its prominent and imposing position at Glasgow Cross was a potent symbol of the growing importance of Glasgow as a trading city.

finest church buildings of its time. The mason, Mungo Naismith, in order to dispel worries over the stability of the massive front portico, is said to have spent the night beneath it following the removal of its supports. The church is currently undergoing conversion to a performance centre, and complementary housing has been built around it to replace the original elegant 18th-century dwellings designed by William Hamilton.

Heading southwards out of the square leads to another intriguing church building, **St Andrew's-by-the-Green** (1750-51), so called because it borders Glasgow Green. Unlike Glasgow's austere Presbyterian churches of the time, this Episcopal church (the first in Scotland) had, among other indulgent luxuries, an organ (now in the St Mungo Museum

There's very little you can't buy at the traditional Glasgow Barras weekend market. Even if you don't intend to make a purchase, it is worth a visit just to soak up the atmosphere.

of Religious Life and Art) which led to its nickname, the 'Kirk o' Whistles'. Like its neighbour, it has now also been converted for office use. In its small burial ground is, among others, the grave of Jane Eliza Madden, 'run over by an omnibus' in 1871.

Bridgegate, to the west of Saltmarket, marks the 12th-century route from High Street down to the River Clyde and, as its name suggests, to the original bridge over the river. Of the many grand buildings which lined this street in the 17th century, the original Merchants' House was the grandest. Only its 17th-century steeple remains, engulfed by the 1873 Fish Market, now the sadly under-utilised Briggait.

Victoria Bridge (1851-54) today crosses that stretch of the Clyde originally spanned by Bishop Rae's medieval Glasgow Bridge of c.1345. To turn back eastwards along Clyde Street leads to the **Judiciary Courts** with their Greek columned façade, in front of which the last public hanging in the city took place in 1865.

Facing the High Court is **Glasgow Green**, the city's and Britain's oldest public park. The entrance to the Green leads through the towering **McLennan Arch** – originally part of the façade of Robert Adam's Assembly

Glasgow's coat of arms features the Bird, the Tree, the Fish and the Bell. Here it is set within a lamp-post outside the People's Palace.

Rooms in Ingram Street. Almost dwarfed by this edifice, the Collins Fountain is significant in its remembrance of the Glasgow publisher Sir William Collins, under whose leadership the European temperance movement began in Glasgow.

A direct route through the park reveals a series of notable monuments and fountains. David Hamilton's **Nelson Monument** (1806) was the first ever to celebrate Nelson's victory at Trafalgar.

Nearby, somewhat insignificantly, but clearly labelled lies a boulder marking the spot where James Watt, on a meditative stroll, is said to have conceived his ideas for the refinement of the steam engine which were to spark off the Industrial Revolution.

The **Doulton Fountain** (1888), dominated by the figure of Queen Victoria, was originally

When he opened the People's Palace in 1898, Lord Rosebery described it as 'a palace of pleasure and imagination around which the people may place their affections.'

the principal Doulton exhibit at the 1888 Empire Exhibition in Kelvingrove Park, presented to the city by Sir Henry Doulton.

The predominant structure on the Green is the wonderful **People's Palace**, a museum devoted to the social and cultural history of Glasgow, and a captivating shrine to the harshness, the opulence, the drive, the despair – all those stark social and cultural contrasts which, existing side by side, have shaped Glasgow's feisty character.

The museum is a veritable treasure trove of artefacts and memorabilia, from Scots artist Ken Currie's bold *Radical Socialist Visions*, to reconstructed shops, to vivid reminiscences of the

Glasgow people illustrated through a range of audio-visual displays. Adjoining the rear of the building is the **Winter Gardens**, a massive glass conservatory bedecked in shrubs and flowers, and the perfect refuge on any rainy day.

Opposite the People's Palace, and the curious forest of poles which symbolises the former practice of Glasgow folk of drying their laundry publicly on Glasgow Green, is one of Glasgow's most

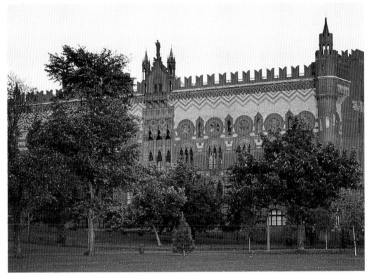

extravagant and eccentric buildings, William Leiper's **Templeton's Carpet Factory** of 1889. Modelled on the Doge's Palace in Venice, it is an exotic assortment of variously coloured brick, circular and pointed windows and sympathetic 1930s extension. The building now operates as the Templeton Business Centre.

Up until the early 1800s, elegant villas bordered Glasgow Green at its north side. With the westwards migration of the wealthy merchants and industrialists, their dwellings disappeared (52 Charlotte Street being one of very few surviving examples). A rather soulless 1980s housing complex stands in their place.

One of Glasgow's architectural curiosities might look like the Venetian Doge's Palace, but this fanciful coloured-brick structure was built originally as a carpet factory for the famous Templeton's company.

THE MERCHANT CITY

The removal of the West Port (or Gate) from the west end of the Trongate in 1751, signalled the development of **Argyle Street**. Now one of Glasgow's main shopping streets, it wasn't always wholly commercial. In the mid 18th century, as the

wealthy merchants turned their backs on the Bridgegate and Saltmarket, some of the first fashionable grand mansions which they built were in Argyle Street, alongside existing single-storey thatched houses.

Its importance as a major thoroughfare increased rapidly with the opening of Jamaica Bridge in 1763, and today's Argyle Street is one of the city's busiest streets. The large, modern **Marks & Spencer's** store on the corner of Virginia Street marks the spot where the once fashionable Black Bull Inn stood. A plaque on the store's Virginia Street wall records a visit by the poet Robert Burns. The site of another famous establishment, the Buck's Head Hotel, is now the location of Alexander 'Greek' Thomson's 1862 **Buck Head Buildings**.

Debenham's (formerly Lewis's) prominent Portland stone department store has an interesting past. John Anderson's Royal Polytechnic originally filled the site between Maxwell Street and Dunlop

Street. When it became a department store in the 1840s it was the first of its kind in Scotland. Lewis's purchased the site in 1925, rebuilding the 'Poly' to create the largest department store in the country.

Opposite Debenham's is one of Scotland's oldest undercover shopping malls, the **Argyll Arcade**, built in 1827 by the architect John Baird, with openings to Argyle Street and Buchanan Street. It owes its simplicity of style to early Parisian models, although its hammer-beam, glass roof structure is thought to be unique among arcade construction. The tenement building which fronts the arcade on Argyle Street is a rare example of how the street's original buildings would have looked.

A major focal point of the street is the **Highlandman's Umbrella** (1901-6), the highly ornamented Central Station viaduct so called because it became a gathering place for immigrant Highlanders looking for work in Glasgow

Just as Argyle Street was short-lived as a truly residential area, so, too, a major building programme to the north of the street was significant, if also ultimately transient – the creation of Glasgow's first New Town, known as the **Merchant City**.

Bounded by Argyle Street in the south, High Street in the east, George Street in the north and Queen Street in the west, the Merchant City retains its basic original block plan and an exciting mixture of buildings (many largely saved and lovingly restored in recent years). The streets are laid out in a Beaux-Arts manner, where significant buildings provide impressive end views to the main thoroughfares.

Ingram Street acts as the spine of the New Town area, running from High Street to Queen Street. At right angles to it run the major Merchant City streets. The **Ramshorn Church** occupies a prominent position at the High Street end, though

◀ *Little remains of the original Trongate buildings immediately west of Glasgow Cross, where the early wealthy merchants would mingle to discuss business. Beyond the Tron Steeple – a part survivor of the original St Mary's Collegiate Church burned down 200 years ago by members of the notorious Hell Fire Club – Argyle Street now forms the link westwards towards today's centre of commerce.*

not so prominent as it used to be, the more recent widening of Ingram Street having removed much of the burial ground at the front. A glance at the pavement reveals a curious set of initials – R F and A F – marking the spot where the Foulis brothers, printers at the University of Glasgow and founders of Glasgow's first School of Art, are buried.

Ramshorn Church, Thomas Rickman's 1824 structure replacing the original 1724 building, no longer operates as such. Like so many buildings in this area, it is now owned by Strathclyde University, who use it as a theatre. Still sacred, however, is the enclosed graveyard to the rear in which, like the Necropolis, are to be found many of Glasgow's worthy merchant names. There, also, lies Pierre Emile L'Angelier, victim of one of Scotland's most famous 'not proven' murder cases, in which Madeleine Smith was accused but not convicted of having poisoned the Frenchman.

The church also provides an imposing end-view looking along the narrow and historic **Candleriggs** from Argyle Street. Originally an area occupied by Glasgow's candlemakers, Candleriggs became the principal market for the city, rather like London's Covent Garden, remaining so until the 1970s. The street has recently been re-landscaped with original cobble stones.

John Cleland's elegant **City Halls** (1817) dominates Candleriggs. The main auditorium, which came into prominence as a concert hall when the St Andrew's Halls burned down in 1962, and equally out of vogue with the opening of the new Glasgow Royal Concert Hall in 1990, was the venue for celebrated lectures and readings by such luminaries as Dickens and Thackeray.

Further west along Ingram Street, past R W Billing's magnificent baronial warehouses (now the residential apartments known as Ingram Square), is the enormous **Sheriff Court Building**. The section of the building nearest Wilson Street, fronted by an immense columned portico, was

▶ *Hutcheson's Hall started life as Hutcheson's Hospital, built with funds from a trust set up by the philanthropic Hutcheson brothers, George and Thomas, to help the poor and needy. Their statues, inset within alcoves on the splendid south-facing façade, originally adorned the tower of an earlier building at the opposite end of Hutcheson Street. Hutcheson's Hall is now owned by the National Trust for Scotland.*

built originally in 1844 as the City and County Buildings. It was extended north to accommodate a new Merchants' House, which faced independently along Garth Street towards its rival institution, the Trades House in Glassford Street. A further addition northwards in 1871 took the building to its present position on Ingram Street. Various abortive proposals for its future use have, as yet, come to nothing.

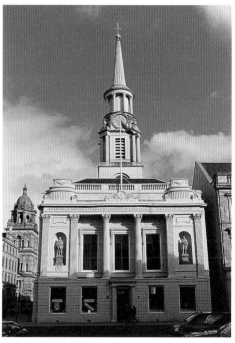

On the opposite side of Ingram Street, facing down Hutcheson Street, the figures of Thomas and George Hutcheson stand proudly within the elevated bays on David Hamilton's 1802 **Hutcheson's Hall**. They predate the building, which began life as Hutcheson's Hospital, having been carved for the original 1655 hospital building which stood at the other end of Hutcheson Street on Trongate. Owned by the National Trust for Scotland, the building houses one of the Trust's shops, and a gloriously decorative hall on the upper floor in which hangs a portrait of Sir William Smith, founder of the Boys' Brigade movement in Glasgow in 1883.

John Street is a pertinent symbol of contemporary Glasgow, its al fresco café as symbolic of the new trendy European city of culture as the **Italian Centre** it forms a part of. Here, Glaswegians enjoy the emporia of Armani and Versace in a setting that combines gritty Victorian façades and Paisley sculptor Alexander Stoddart's neo-classical statues, with ultra modern chic. Even the sacred portals of J T Rochead's **John Street Church** (1859-60) operate these days as a pub!

The most significant building on Glassford Street is Robert Adam's 1794 **Trades House**, as old as the street itself, and the second oldest building in Glasgow still operating in its original function. The view along Garth Street from the old

Restoration and refurbishment in Glasgow's Merchant City have revitalised an area of the city which, by the 1970s, was run down and neglected.

Merchants' House shows the Trades House at its best, from its pedimented first floor to the fine mouldings (carvings of the City's arms) and simple green dome. The interior is well worth a look, particularly the magnificent pilastered Banqueting Hall with its carved wooden ceiling.

When domestic mansions were no longer in vogue in the Merchant City, banks and civic buildings took their place. The beautiful, domed **TSB** building is a gem, as is the lavishly ornamented **Lanarkshire House** (with six wonderful statues by Mossman), a reworking by John Burnet of David Hamilton's 1841 former Union Bank, itself a replacement of Virginia Mansion.

Virginia Street – which began life as one of Britain's oldest banking sites – houses yet another remnant of the area's trading tradition, **Crown Arcade**, a glass-roofed galleried hall used originally as a tobacco and, later, sugar exchange. The ground floor is no longer as it was originally, but the hollow wooden columns dating from 1819 when Crown Arcade was built remain on the first floor. Nowadays, the Virginia Antique Galleries operate here as well as in neighbouring buildings. Among the best of the street's second-generation architecture which still survives today is the building opposite on the corner of Wilson Street, now a hotel, which still has its original turnpike stair to the rear.

Once a tobacco merchant's mansion, then the Royal Exchange, then a library, this is now Glasgow's Gallery of Modern Art

All but one of the original detached villas which once lined **Miller Street** have disappeared over the years. The recent restoration of No. 42, built by John Craig in 1775 and known as the **Tobacco Merchant's House**, is a delightful example of how elegant the street once looked.

Ingram Street's crowning glory is the huge portico of Corinthian columns which fronts the **Gallery of Modern Art** at the Queen Street end.

The building itself has undergone considerable changes in character and usage over the years. It started life as one of Glasgow's most prestigious mansions, built for the Tobacco Lord, John Cunninghame, who sold it to the Royal Bank in 1817. When it moved into the hands of the Royal Exchange ten years later, David Hamilton was enlisted to reface the mansion, add the frontage, and the 130-foot vaulted hall to the rear which, at the time, was the daily gathering place for Glasgow's businessmen.

The building later housed Stirling's Library (before its return to Miller Street), and in 1996 re-emerged as the new controversial Gallery of Modern Art. Spread over four floors, each gallery takes as its theme one of the four natural elements: Earth; Air; Water; and Fire. The range of exhibits, many by Scottish artists, is both entertaining and challenging, and the use of interactive displays – for children of all ages! – makes it extremely popular for families. Adding to the rooftop dining experience is the colourful Adrian Wisniewski mural which covers the walls of the cafeteria.

The recent re-landscaping of the surrounding **Royal Exchange Square** – where the mysterious Glasgow tradition of placing a traffic cone on top of the statue of Wellington continues, and open-air diners mingle (sometimes nervously) with fast-moving skate-boarders – has revitalised this western edge of the Merchant City, and enhanced the route through the square towards Buchanan Street.

It is hard to believe that the busy city centre street now called Queen Street was once the main cattle drovers' route into Glasgow, and the quiet thoroughfare by which Oliver Cromwell entered the city in 1650 to avoid the potential trouble he might have encountered from opposing factions based at the Bishop's Castle.

It is equally hard to envisage **George Square**, which Queen Street spills into at its north end, as a gentle grazing ground for sheep. Even when it was

▶ *Despite the modern office building and unwieldy hotel extension on its northern boundary, George Square has maintained its stately presence as the municipal heart of modern-day Glasgow. Established at the north-west corner of the Merchant City in the late 18th century, and originally bordered by hotels and mansions, it is now dominated by the wonderful Victorian City Chambers.*

properly laid out in 1781, the water-filled square remained a popular spot for drowning cats and dogs and slaughtering horses. Some say, with the city's council headquarters now in the Square's magnificent City Chambers, that such a tradition should be revived – this time using political animals!

Today's George Square is the city's true focal point for civic and commercial matters, and the spot which the people of Glasgow rightly call their city centre.

On a sunny day, many office workers, students, tourists, and the ever-hungry and expectant pigeons pack the square around lunchtime, mingling with the statues of Queen Victoria and Prince Albert, Robert Burns, William Gladstone, Robert Peel, Sir John Moore and Lord Clyde, among other more parochial worthies. A robust and stalky cenotaph graces the east end.

At the centre of the Square is a column supporting not, as you would expect, George III (the consequences of his failure with the American Colonies rather soured his reputation with Glasgow's tobacco merchants), but the figure of Sir Walter Scott. Who else but a literary figure for a City of Culture?

Of the buildings, the **Copthorne Hotel** is, despite its many alterations, the sole survivor of several hotels which initially dominated George Square. Unfortunately, a modern extension to its west gable screens off the fan-glassed canopy of **Queen Street Station** so much admired by John Betjeman. Equally undeserving of their prime city-centre position are the stark modern accountancy offices on the north-east corner.

▶ Glasgow's Renaissance-style City Chambers, completed in 1888 by the architect William Young, is undoubtedly one of Britain's finest and grand-est town halls. Like many of Glasgow's fine buildings it can be viewed equally well at night thanks to an extensive city-wide floodlighting programme. The bulky stone cenotaph in front is the location for the city's annual Remembrance Day ceremony.

Many of the Square's original hotels occupied the graceful symmetrical terrace along the west side. That symmetry has gone, albeit tastefully, as a result of the heightened north section which houses today's **Merchants' House** (1874-77, John Burnet). Among its bold external features are hefty carved figures supporting the corner bays, and a towering dome capped by a merchant ship under full sail. Inside, the stately Merchants' Hall bears the wall-mounted commemorative boards of its wealthy benefactors.

The **Tourist Information Centre** occupies the refurbished Moncrieff House on the south side. An Orientation Centre on the second floor gives visitors a useful taster of the city's attractions and facilities.

The City Chambers, built in Italian Renaissance style (1883-8, William Young), has grandeur and quality in its every detail. Within a framework of tiered Classical columns, domed corner turrets, and a magnificent central tower, the façade contains a wealth of sculptural details and tableaux including, above the central pediment, the figure of Queen Victoria. It was she who opened the building in 1888.

Inside, the entrance vestibule is a direct statement of Glasgow's confidence and wealth, furnished in Venetian mosaics, granite pillars capped with rich Italian marble, and elegantly vaulted domes.

Of the two routes to the upper suites, the grand marble staircase is luxuriant to the last, around which domes, arches and vaults in various coloured marble and alabaster form an elaborate concoction. Every room has its own distinct character. The Council Chamber, in Spanish mahogany, is dark and dignified with a magnificent linen-backed frieze of Tynecastle tapestry. Of a lighter hue is the richly wooded Satinwood Room and the adjoining Octagonal Room. Beautiful as they are, they hardly prepare you for the sumptuous grandeur of the massive Banqueting Hall.

Size is everything here. A sparkling array of chandeliers illuminate walls adorned with enormous murals. Along the south wall are three glorious examples by Glasgow artists: Alexander der Roche's depiction of St Mungo's miracle of the salmon and the ring; Edward Walton's *Glasgow Fair*; and Sir John Lavery's gutsy portrayal of early industry on the River Clyde.

On exiting this elaborate municipal palace, a backward glance at the pediment over the entrance reveals the city's motto, 'Let Glasgow Flourish'. The City Chambers is a living symbol that, by the end of the 19th century, it surely had.

CITY CENTRE

As George Square established itself as the new hub of municipal life in Glasgow, the city swiftly spread further west, creating, in effect, a second New Town characterised by a strict geometric grid layout – rather like New York in miniature.

Leaving George Square at its south-west corner leads along **St Vincent Place**, a short, broader stretch of St Vincent Street bordered by a rich variety of Victorian Renaissance buildings, to the junction with Buchanan Street.

At the south end of Buchanan Street – across Argyle Street – is **St Enoch Square**, dominated by the St Enoch Centre, a colossal glass-roofed modern shopping complex, impressive enough for its kind, but an entirely different concept from the grand St Enoch Railway Station and Hotel it replaced. The area remains a focal point for local transport, Glasgow's noisey buses vying with the pigeons for the attention of shoppers and travellers. The **Travel Centre**, a delightfully miniature, turreted Jacobean building, erected in 1896 originally as part of the equally diminutive Glasgow Underground system, commands a distinctive position in the centre of the Square.

Buchanan Street is the city's foremost shopping street for range and quality. Top name outlets and department stores line the pedestrianised thoroughfare, but there are a few wonderful surprises.

A narrow lane close to the Argyll Arcade entrance leads to an attractive secluded courtyard and **Sloan's Restaurant**, reputedly Glasgow's oldest, and once a highly popular venue for afternoon tea dances.

Princes Square is Buchanan Street's real jewel in the crown. A former enclosed courtyard, now elegantly glass-roofed, it is undoubtedly Glasgow's most chic multi-floored shopping mall with an exclusive range of specialist shops and appetising mix of formal and less formal eating places. Its

▶ *It is hard to imagine that the tasteful glass-covered Princes Square was once an underused open backstreet courtyard. Today it is one of Glasgow's most fashionable shopping malls, with an exhaustive choice of informal eating outlets. It forms part of the more exclusive range of shops to be found along Buchanan Street.*

mosaic-covered ground floor is a hive of activity, often featuring entertainers, artists or exhibitions.

A sideways step off Buchanan Street, along Mitchell Lane, reveals one of Glasgow's many fine examples of buildings by Charles Rennie Mackintosh. The former **Glasgow Herald Building** (1893-95) in Mitchell Street (the newspaper moved to Albion Street some years ago) has many of Mackintosh's hallmarks. This is most prominent in the ornamental wrought iron work and in the distinctive octagonal print tower which dominates the view down West Nile street. It has now been refurbished and reopened as **The Lighthouse**, Scotland's Centre for Design and Architecture.

Along Gordon Street a glimpse of the Venetian-styled **Ca'd'oro** building (1872, John Honeyman) is recommended. Its slim cast-iron bays with Corinthian shafts sit gracefully above the giant masonry arches at street level. At the west end of the street is the grand frontage and bold clock tower of the Central Hotel, built in 1879 by the Glasgow and South Western Railway to outclass its rival company's St Enoch Hotel. Central Station, itself, has a noble countenance within, its stylish wooden frontages elegantly planned and delightfully aesthetic.

More hidden Mackintosh lies along the narrow Renfield Lane and the former offices of the **Daily Record** newspaper (1901). Its tall, white brick structure deserves a more spacious setting where details typical of Mackintosh could be better appreciated.

The **Horse Shoe Bar** in Drury Street (off Renfield Street) holds one undisputed record – or at least there are very few who would be brave enough to question its claim to have the longest continuous bar in Europe.

Back in Buchanan Street, a cluster of fine buildings grace the area around **Nelson Mandela Place** (formerly St George's Place). At the centre is **St George's Tron Church** (1807, William Stark), dominated by its soaring obelisk-topped tower.

The French Gothic **Stock Exchange** (1875, John Burnet) is undoubtedly one of the city's finest buildings. It is worth just catching a glimpse of its reflection in the modern Clydesdale Bank building opposite, where the rippling effects of the glass exaggerate the filigree ornamentation.

On the north-west corner of the square, **The Royal Faculty of Procurators** (1854, Charles Wilson) is a fine example of the many Venetian Renaissance-style buildings in Glasgow. Its sculpted stonework portrays local eminent legal figures, while inside is a grand arch-lined library.

On the adjacent **Athenaeum** building (1885, J J Burnet), Mossman's carved figures of Flaxman, Purcell, Wren and Reynolds perched on its topmost ledge allude to its former use as part of the Royal Scottish Academy of Music and Drama, a role it shared with the adjoining red sandstone corner building (originally A N Paterson's 1909 Liberal Club), and the further adjoining **Athenaeum Theatre** (1891-3, J J Burnet) on Buchanan Street.

▶ *The Royal Scottish Automobile Club – a stylish remodelling of John Brash's original classical west-facing terrace – forms the entire east side of Blythswood Square. It is also one of four complementary terraces which make this hilltop square, with fenced off central gardens, one of the city's most graceful and attractive.*

A moderately steep walk up West George Street, from the west flank of Nelson Mandela Square, leads to one of Glasgow's most elegant and complete squares. In its elevated position, **Blythswood Square** has at its centre a spacious garden surrounded by four identical classical terraces by John Brash (1823-29), the most impressive of these being the **Royal Scottish Automobile Club** on the east side, the central

porch entrance of which was added in 1923.

The square has its idiosyncrasies. The 1908 door inset to No.5 is by Charles Rennie Mackintosh, and the lady who once lived next door (No.7) was none other than Madeleine Smith who, in 1857, stood trial for the murder of her French lover Pierre Emile L'Angelier. The verdict was a peculiarly Scottish one – 'Not Proven' – enabling Madeleine to go free. L'Angelier is buried in the Ramshorn Graveyard.

Close inspection of the **Malmaison Hotel**, over the brow of the hill, reveals its former ecclesiastical existence as St Jude's (1838-9, John Stephen), a stalky Greek Revival church redeveloped and extended to its current use in the early 1990s.

On St Vincent Street, to the south of the square, is a building which could easily be mistaken for an ancient Greek temple – Alexander 'Greek' Thomson's **St Vincent Street Church** (1858-9). The vividly coloured interior would itself be stunning, were it not for an exterior which stands fortress-like over Bothwell Street, and whose prominent tower is heavily bedecked with rich neo-classical motifs.

Over Bath Street to the north of Blythswood Square, **Sauchiehall Street** (meaning 'meadow of willows') runs from Glasgow Royal Concert Hall at the top of Buchanan Street, deep into the city's west end. The **Royal Concert Hall** is relatively new, built in 1990 to a design by Sir Norman Foster and opened as part of the European City of Culture celebrations. Its 2000-seater auditorium is Glasgow's principal venue for mainstream classical and popular light music entertainment. The massive adjoining new **Buchanan Galleries** retail centre, built with similar white sandstone cladding, opened in 1999.

A stroll up Sauchiehall Street, particularly to shop, can be thirsty work, which is probably one reason why the rather special **Willow Tea Rooms** are so popular. The other reason is, of course, that this fashionable spot for morning coffee or afternoon tea is the only remaining example of one of several tea rooms designed by Mackintosh for Miss Kate Cranston.

Nowadays, with tea sipping only on the upper floor, entrance is via the ground floor jewellers' shop. But the real jewel is the 'Room De Luxe' itself, where bright horizontal windows admit shafts of bright light onto the original fittings and furnishings of Mackintosh and his wife, Margaret Macdonald.

Coach builder, cathedral restorer and art collector, Archibald McLellan, who bequeathed his considerable art collection to the city, also gave his name to the imposing suite of buildings which now houses Glasgow's principal venue for visiting

▶ *Among the architectural curiosities lining the Charing Cross end of Sauchiehall Street is the Baird Hall. This striking example of 1930s art deco began life as a hotel aimed at attracting visitors to the Empire Exhibition, and today is one of the student halls of residence for Strathclyde University. Towering to ten storeys, its original multi-coloured tiling, now largely obscured, must have been a sight to behold.*

exhibitions. The **McLellan Galleries** (1855, James Smith) occupy the site between Rose Street and Dalhousie Street.

The area surrounding this part of Sauchiehall Street has often been said to contain Glasgow's 'string of cultural pearls'. At the top of Hope Street, the **Theatre Royal**, with its sumptuously restored interior (C J Phipps, 1895) is the present home to Scottish Opera and Scottish Ballet.

Opposite, on Renfrew Street, is the new red brick **Royal Scottish Academy of Music and Drama** (1985, Sir Norman Foster), Scotland's principal performing arts conservatoire. In honour of one of Glasgow's greatest musical sons, Sir Alexander Gibson, a new Opera School

bearing his name opened in 1999. The nearby **Piping Centre** (formerly Cowcaddens United Free Church) not only provides a venue for bagpipe study and events, but houses a piping museum, restaurant and adjoining hotel.

For traditional popular Glasgow entertainment, the twin-towered **Pavilion Theatre** (1902-3, Bertie Crewe) has long fitted the bill. Over the years, its delightful French interior has echoed to the laughs of many a pantomime season. Where Renfrew Street enters the raised area of **Garnethill**, the corner building of Scandinavian influence on Rose Street, erected in 1939 as the Cosmo Cinema, is now the acclaimed **Glasgow Film Theatre**.

A few hundred yards up Renfrew Street, raised high above the rear of the McLellan Galleries, is Charles Rennie Mackintosh's acknowledged masterpiece, the **Glasgow School of Art**. Completed in 1909, it is a lasting testament to his creative ingenuity given the astonishingly difficult site on which it is built.

The frontage onto Renfrew Street is dominated by massive window blocks (a practical measure to ensure plenty of natural light enters the teaching rooms) and subtle ornamental wrought iron work with its characteristic Mackintosh floral motifs. The western elevation creates a striking vertical sensation achieved by narrow grilled windows which rise over the entire three storeys.

The interior makes highly individual use of dark wood, particularly in the famous Library, where filtered light effects create a warm and relaxed atmosphere. The Mackintosh Room, with its unique furniture, and the Museum containing Mackintosh's drawings and other material, should not be missed.

Further along Renfrew Street is one of Britain's oldest Jewish churches, **Garnethill Synagogue** (1881, John McLeod), easily spotted by its prominent Romanesque doorway leading to an interior that is strikingly original.

Also untouched is Glasgow's most famous time-capsule, the **Tenement House** on Buccleuch Street. The first-floor flat, built in 1892, was inhabited between 1911 and 1965 by a dressmaker, Miss Agnes Toward, who had a habit of never throwing anything away. When she died, her niece recognised the importance of the flat and its quaint historical contents. The National Trust for Scotland took ownership and it is now one of Glasgow's most intriguing testaments to the life of an ordinary lady.

Back on Sauchiehall Street, the **Royal Highland Fusiliers Museum** celebrates the history of a regiment famous for the record number of honours it received in battle.

The **Centre for Contemporary Arts**, temporarily resited at the McLellan Galleries for refurbishment in 1999, is one of the city's most adventurous arts venues, which is housed in the equally fascinating 'Greek' Thomson Grecian Chambers. Further west is the soaring art deco **Baird Hall**, now halls of residence for Strathclyde University, but built originially in 1938 as the Beresford Hotel. The architects, Weddell & Inglis, gave it a cinema façade specifically to attract business!

Charing Cross marks the western perimeter of the city centre area. Very little of its original character remains, having been sliced apart by the M8 motorway which runs east to Edinburgh. But Burnet's **Charing Cross Mansions** (1889-91) offer a hint of the soft, refined elegance that is a feature of the city's nearby fashionable west end.

◀ *Hailed as Charles Rennie Mackintosh's greatest masterpiece, the Glasgow School of Art sums up the marvellous synthesis of influences which the celebrated art nouveau architect and designer achieved in all of his work. Besides the rugged Scottish stone character, distinctive European elegance is evident in the Art School's fenestration and iron work.*

ALONG THE RIVER CLYDE

For centuries, the River Clyde remained a broad and shallow river, dotted with islands and sand banks. When finally the city hit upon a solution in the 18th century to overcome its shallowness, making it navigable to merchant and passenger ships, Glasgow's status and wealth expanded instantly. Nowadays, those few boats that do sail its upper stretches can only venture as far as the Kingston Bridge, yet the river remains a prominent, if more tranquil, feature of the city.

Along its banks at **Glasgow Green** (see p.25) the only vessels you will see nowadays are those belonging to the members of Glasgow Rowing Club. The view of the river eastwards from Albert Bridge (at the west end of Glasgow Green), where mature trees overhang its banks, is exquisite.

Albert Bridge marks the start of the **Clyde Walkway**, a pathway on the north bank running westwards parallel to Clyde Street. It also forms the first of several major bridges which connect the city centre with the south side.

En route to Victoria Bridge – the location of Glasgow's first medieval crossing – is the city's famous flea market, **Paddy's Market**, set between the **Judiciary Courts** and the **Briggait** (see p.25) in the somewhat foreboding alleyway formed by the bridge supports which once took trains into St Enoch Station.

The glinting oriental tower on the opposite bank marks the position of Glasgow's **Central Mosque**, a stunning sight and a symbol of the city's large Moslem population.

Beyond Victoria Bridge stands something of a modern day folly. The 1980s apartments on the north bank were named Carrick Quay on the basis that they looked directly out onto the **M.V. *Carrick***, a former tea clipper which for many years lay moored on the Clyde. Severe weather damaged the ship, and it was removed down river for

◄ From Glasgow Green westwards a series of road, rail and pedestrian bridges crosses the River Clyde linking the north and the south of the city. A considerable amount of improved landscaping and cleaning up of its banks has given the riverside area a more attractive appeal in recent years.

preservation. It has never returned.

One of Clyde Street's principal landmarks is the impressive Gothic structure of **St Andrew's Cathedral**, designed by James Gillespie Graham and consecrated in 1816 to meet the needs of the city's growing Roman Catholic population. Framed by splendid buttresses and turrets, the riverside façade is crowned by an inset statue of St Andrew.

The cathedral looks across the river to one of the finest Classical terraces in the city. **Carlton Place**, designed by Peter Nicholson in 1804 and known as Glasgow's Harley Street for most of the 19th century, is the best surviving example of a larger new town development planned, but never fully completed, for the area.

From Carlton Place, access across the river is by Alexander Kirkland's **Suspension Bridge**, built originally in 1851-3, but later strengthened due to fears over its stability. Kirkland's sturdy Greek supports frame the bridge's 400-foot span.

Near the north end of the bridge is John Taylor's recognisable Doric-columned **Custom House Building** of 1840, with its ornately sculptured coat of arms and sympathetic 20th-century additions to either side.

A trio of bridges darken the Clyde's waters at the foot of Jamaica Street. **Jamaica Bridge**, itself, was originally constructed in 1833 by Thomas Telford, and although substantially widened and reconstructed, much of Telford's granite facings and ballustrade remain. The highest of the bridges is the main **Central Station Viaduct** into Glasgow's principal railway station. Note the solid Dalbeattie granite piers which are remnants of the original 1878 three-span bridge. Completed in 1924, **George V Bridge** is the most recent of the three structures.

Beyond this point Clyde Street becomes the **Broomielaw**, the site of Glasgow's first harbour. Its most notable building is appropriately linked to this maritime tradition. The grandeur and

► *For many years, following its heyday as a major trading port, Glasgow turned its back on the river that had helped make its fortune. With the decline in river-based commerce, the areas along the Broomielaw and Clyde Street fell into neglect. But attention has focused once again on the Clyde, this time as a place of peace and relaxation.*

opulence of the 1882 **Clyde Port Authority** building is a telling indication of how powerful and influential the former Clyde Navigation Trust was, its frontage dominated by a giant statue of Neptune, and its entrance topped by stone carved boats which literally emerge from the main structure. Its interior is equally impressive.

One vessel moored on the river at this point, performs a quite different function from its

intended use. The old **Renfrew Ferry** now provides a fashionable venue for ceilidhs, festive events, and private functions.

On the south side of the river, where the rather utilitarian concrete span of the Kingston Bridge constantly roars with traffic, is a building whose design origins go some way to explaining its ostentatious proportions. The grand Renaissance structure that was the warehouse headquarters of the **Scottish Co-operative Society** started life as an unsuccessful entry for the City Chambers competition.

To the west of the **Kingston Bridge**, running along the north bank, is Anderston Quay, which is the main embarkation point for the **P S** *Waverley*, the world's oldest sea-going paddle steamer which takes passengers on regular 'doon the watter' summer day cruises, visiting the main Clyde Estuary resorts of Greenock, Dunoon, Largs, Rothesay and Millport.

The **Finnieston Crane** is a haunting monument

to the city's great industrial past. Built in the 1930s, it was the largest of its type in Europe, hoisting locomotives which had started life in Glasgow's Springburn Works and would now travel by sea to the far reaches of the Empire.

A clue to the original role of the curious circular **North Rotunda**, now a casino and restaurants, lies in the identical structure visible across the river. These were the original entrance points to the

The Finnieston Crane once hoisted locomotives built at nearby Springburn onto ships to be exported all over the world.

old Harbour Tunnel, built in 1895, and often used for moving cattle from one side of the river to the other. The South Rotunda, used as an exhibition space in the early 1990s, currently lies vacant.

The large modern complex occupying the old Queen Elizabeth Docks area is Glasgow's premier conference and exhibition centre. The most recent addition to the **Scottish Exhibition and Confer-**

ence Centre is also its most outstanding feature, the easily recognisable '**Armadillo**'. Opened in 1997, this 3000-seater conference auditorium gained its pet name from the giant interweaving metal roof sections which resemble the armadillo's scaled back. The glass skyscraper alongside is the Glasgow **Moat House Hotel**, Scotland's tallest hotel structure with panoramic views from its scenic external elevator.

Bell's Bridge is easily identified by its modern and colourful presence. First built as a pedestrian walkway across the river to the highly successful and popular **1988 Garden Festival** site, it now opens regularly to allow river vessels to pass through.

Currently unused, the former Garden Festival site is now undergoing considerable redevelopment, the focus of which will be a new Glasgow **Science Centre**. In line with the times, the Clyde and its surrounding banks have been transformed from a noisy and busy industrial heartland to become a more tranquil, cleaner landscape where leisure and recreation are foremost.

Echoes of Sydney Opera House on the Clyde. Glasgow's new 3000-seater conference centre – known affectionately as the 'Armadillo' – opened in 1997.

WEST END

Charing Cross marks a critical crossing-over point in Glasgow, from the busy city centre to the more douce and refined Kelvingrove and University areas. Little remains of the original buildings which enclosed its hectic junction. Of those that do, the elaborate and decorative **Charing Cross Mansions** reflect the former grand status of the Cross. It is largely now a vehicular labyrinth bereft of its soul.

A delightful little curiosity remains, however, in the **Cameron Memorial Fountain** which sits at the corner of Sauchiehall Street and North Street. Known as 'the leaning fountain', regular checks since its characteristic list was first noticed in 1926 have revealed a gradually increasing tilt to the east.

Night or day you can't miss the glorious dome of the **Mitchell Library**, also on North Street. This great Renaissance palace of literature, erected in 1911 by W B Whitie, houses Europe's largest reference collection. Originally founded in 1877 by the Tobacco Lord Stephen Mitchell, the library has one of the finest Burns collections, with many of the poet's first editions and a host of memorabilia. Its fascinating **Glasgow Room** is undoubtedly the central point of reference for all matters relating to the city's history.

Equally fascinating, and easy to miss, is the façade at the rear of the building on Granville Street. The giant sculpted figures by Mossman – of Mozart, Beethoven, Michelangelo and others – which adorn its impressive frontage are a clue to the fact that this was once the St Andrew's Halls, Glasgow's foremost concert hall, gutted by fire in 1962. Internally rebuilt, it is now part of the Mitchell Library, incorporating the Mitchell Theatre.

On the sloping hill to the north of Sauchiehall Street as it heads west from Charing Cross, is the

◄ *The magnificent tower of Sir George Gilbert Scott's Glasgow University building dominates the city's West End sky-line, rising high above its hilltop position at the north side of Kelvingrove Park. Visitors to the University can walk up the tower and enjoy one of the finest panoramic views of Glasgow. The long climb up the many narrow steps is well worth it.*

wonderfully preserved architecture of the **Park Conservation Area**, and at its very peak, the magnificent curved line of French-roofed terraced houses, now mainly used as offices, which make up Park Circus.

Also dominating the skyline are the lean Italianate towers of the former **Trinity College**, now exclusive apartments, and the more squat tower belonging to what was **Park Parish Church**, now

Standing high above the valley of the River Kelvin, the gentle sweep of Park Circus is a truly wonderful sight – Glasgow at its opulent Victorian best.

modern offices ingeniously constructed around the original tower.

Over the hill, on Woodlands Road, is a more recent monument to a peculiarly Glasgow fictional character, **Lobey Dosser**. The hero of a cartoon strip created by Bud Neal in 1949 for the local evening newspaper, Lobey is depicted astride his two-legged horse El Fideldo, presumably in pursuit of his evil opponent Rank Bajin!

From the elevated position of Woodlands Terrace, the **Roberts Memorial**, a regal equestrian bronze statue, marks the start of the grand descent from the Park area to La Belle Place via Charles Wilson's monumental grand staircase of 1853. The same

architect's heavily friezed **Queen's Rooms** (now
the Christian Science Church) occupies a prominent position at the foot of the hill.

As Sauchiehall Street takes a slight kink to the
right, past the elegant geometrical consistency of
Alexander Taylor's 1839 **Royal Crescent**, the vista
opens spectacularly to reveal the open spaces and
cultural treasures of the Kelvingrove area.

Kelvingrove Park, itself, can be entered from

the Park Circus area, and contains a wealth of
interesting monuments and sculpture, including
the heavily ornamented **Stewart Memorial
Fountain**. The Lady of the Lake, perched in
bronze at the very top of the monument, symbolises the advent of Glasgow's newly developed
water supply from Loch Katrine, introduced during
Stewart's tenure as the city's Lord Provost.

As the park crosses the River Kelvin and reaches
Kelvin Way, two further monumental structures
are well worth inspection: the sturdy statue of
Thomas Carlyle, whose head and shoulders
emerge almost organically from a solid rock
plinth; and the seated bronze statue of Glasgow

*Beyond
St George's
Mansions at the
start of Wood-
lands Road, the
vista takes in
the dramatic
spires and
rooftops which
dominate the
city's west side.*

University's most famous physicist, **Lord Kelvin**.

The west side of the park is dominated by the magnificently ornate **Glasgow Art Gallery and Museum**, built in 1901 to a Renaissance concept by Sir J W Simpson and Milner Allen. Clusters of spires and towers crown a red sandstone construction that achieves exactly what it was intended to do, to send a message throughout the world that Glasgow was wealthy, cultured and successful.

There is a story, with no basis in fact, that the building was mistakenly constructed back to front, and that the architect subsequently threw himself from its turrets. It's a good story, if nothing else!

It is a veritable palace of art, containing the city's principal collection of paintings by the great Dutch and Italian Renaissance masters, and a wonderful range of Impressionist works. Some of the finest examples of Rembrandt, Botticelli, Monet and Picasso adorn the walls of its airy halls and picture promenade gallery. A display called 'Glasgow 1900' sets Charles Rennie Mackintosh and his contemporaries in the context of *fin de siècle* Glasgow, with examples of paintings, furniture and decorative arts. In recent years the city's arts leaders have freshened up the gallery by introducing staged exhibitions and events, including the relaxed and informal recitals which utilise the great central hall's mighty restored Lewis organ.

Across Dumbarton Road, and along the side road which follows the River Kelvin, is the **Museum of Transport**. Its open and expansive interior holds a wonderful array of historical vehicles and carriages which make it highly popular with family groups.

Glasgow trams, displaying astonishing examples of quality workmanship, trolley buses, full-size locomotives in pristine condition, royal railway carriages, fire engines, motor and pedal bicycles, and even Sir William Burrell's own limousine, are among the many fine exhibits.

In one corner of the museum a faithfully reconstructed 1930s Glasgow cobbled street has its own cinema (showing archive Glasgow footage), electrical shop, post office, newspaper booth, and even an underground station. Glasgow's 'Subway' system, a simple and diminutive circular underground railway covering the city centre, west end and south side of the river, remains one of the most efficient ways to travel around the city.

A more profound nostalgia trip awaits in the **Clyde Room** which houses Glasgow's splendid collection of model ships, most but not all of their full-size counterparts built on the River Clyde. Among them, and revealing the same astounding detail, are the famous Cunard Queens – the *Queen Mary*, *Queen Elizabeth*, and *QE2*. Even the Clyde-built former Royal yacht *Britannia* has a proud place within the display cases, despite east-coast rival Leith's recent coup in securing the real thing!

The Museum of Transport shares the vast shell that once was the city's principal exhibition centre with the **Kelvin Hall International Sports Arena**, a fully equipped track and sports facility which regularly stages international indoor competitions.

◀ *Glasgow Art Gallery and Museum in Kelvingrove is the city's flagship gallery, attracting around a million visitors each year. Like the majority of the city's galleries and museums, entry is free. So it is possible to visit its wonderful collection time after time, and enjoy the Rembrandts, Botticellis, Monets and Picassos and much more at your leisure.*

The view north from Partick Bridge following the tree-covered route of the River Kelvin focuses at its height on the majestic spread of the **University of Glasgow** main building. Undoubtedly one of Sir George Gilbert Scott's finest designs, erected between 1866-86, the University could hardly have picked a more prominent position than Gilmorehill for its move away from the Old College on High Street. The soaring Flemish spire is a significant landmark even from distant vantage points outwith the city.

The common approach to the University is from University Avenue, stretching from the far end of Kelvin Way over the brow of the hill to Byres Road. One of its gate houses, **Pearce Lodge**, at the bottom end of the avenue, is a legacy from the original University, transferred and rebuilt in 1870.

The main building has a bright new **Visitor Centre** on the ground floor. Stairways on either side of the building's central protruding apse lead to the double quadrangle, from which access can be gained to the University's finest internal features.

The rib-vaulted cloisters which divide the east and west quadrangles also support the **Bute Hall**, the University's principal grand assembly hall and venue for its graduations. Inside, the slender wrought-iron columns are decorated with blue and gold fleur-de-lys, and the fine windows depict leading world figures.

Beyond a glorious wooden screen is the **Randolph Hall** with portraits by Reynolds and Raeburn.

From the adjacent **Professors' Square** – as its name implies, originally built as homes for the senior staff – it is possible to enter the University's **Memorial Chapel** via the **Lion and Unicorn Stairway**, an original part of the Old College, moved to its current spot in 1872.

To the north of the Bute Hall is the **Hunterian Museum**, Scotland's oldest museum collection, put together in 1807. Its benefactor, Sir William

▶ *One of the most fascinating tributes to Charles Rennie Mackintosh is the faithful reconstruction of his nearby Southpark Avenue house within Glasgow University's Hunterian Art Gallery. Its three storeys are neatly laid out with his fittings and furnishings. In the attic space are further exhibits representing his unique work, including a reconstruction of the famous blue Derngate bedroom.*

Hunter (the famous London anatomist and physicist who received his early education at the University), was an avid collector of coins, and these form part of the collection alongside archaeological and ethnographic material and exhibits related to his own line of work.

On the other side of University Avenue, adjacent to the modern high-rise library, is the **Hunterian Art Gallery**, another wonderful attraction owing

its existence to Hunter. Its well-lit gallery shows off paintings by Chardin, Rembrandt, Hockney and Charles Rennie Mackintosh, at their best; but in particular, the building houses one of the most important collections of work by the American artist James MacNeill Whistler.

However, what most people flock here to see is the superb reconstruction of Mackintosh's house (originally situated in what is now nearby South-park Avenue) which covers four floors and features many of the unique furnishings and fittings which graced the famous Glasgow architect and designer's home. Just don't exit by the front door. As close examination from the exterior will reveal, it is purely cosmetic and a sheer drop awaits!

Byres Road is the hub of Glasgow's trendy West End, its pubs and restaurants – and those set back in its various alleyways – are favourite haunts of the many students and young people who live in the area. At its top end it meets the Great Western Road, the city's main route west to Loch Lomond and the Trossachs.

Great Western Road is long, broad and very

Botanic Gardens in Glasgow's West End provide a peaceful haven on the edge of the busy city. Its original purpose was to provide medicinal plants for Glasgow University.

straight. Near its city-centre end is another Sir George Gilbert Scott (and son, John Oldrid Scott) creation, **St Mary's Episcopal Cathedral** (1893), its spire with full bell tower both visible and audible local landmarks. Another spire, that of **Lands-downe Church**, competes in the skyline. Someone wrote of John Honeyman's 1862 design as being 'perhaps the most attractive Victorian Gothic church in the city.' Certainly, occupying a spot high above the plunging valley of the River Kelvin, it is spectacularly positioned.

A cluster of buildings across the cast-iron structure of Kelvin Bridge deserve mention. The extravagant **Caledonian Mansions** (1897, James Miller) were originally built as an annexe to the Central Hotel, served by the branch line to Kelvingrove Station. The delightful art deco building opposite, formerly the **City Bakeries**, is notable for its prominent terracotta facing.

At the junction with Byres Road and Queen Margaret Drive is the entrance to one of Glasgow's most peaceful and beautiful havens, the **Botanic Gardens**. At its centre is the stunning Kibble Palace, essentially a glass temple in which are grown exotic flowers, orchids in particular. Often used as a venue for concerts and other public events, it simply oozes Victoriana.

Across Queen Margaret Drive is the collection of buildings which make up **BBC Scotland's** head-quarter studios. Its most interesting section is that which faces on to Queen Margaret Drive, the Italianate palazzo building originally built as a private art gallery, then to become a Ladies' College.

In a city noted for its magnificent Victorian architecture, even the doorways of residential properties, like this Hillhead flat, have a character and fascination of their own.

Great Western Road continues its westward route lined by elegant terraces and handsome villas (including the former Glasgow home of Sir William Burrell) until it finally reaches **Anniesland Cross**, officially recognised as one of Britain's most complex city junctions. The easiest manoeuvre is a left turn towards the Clyde, where another of Glasgow's many parks offers a further surprise. Within **Victoria Park** is **Fossil Grove**, a fascinating display of fossilised tree stumps dating back hundreds of millions of years, not so much placed there as uncovered during local construction work several years ago.

THE NORTHERN EDGE

From several access points in the west of the city, the scenic **Kelvin Walkway** follows the River Kelvin, particularly on its route north west past the **Forth and Clyde Canal** and **Kelvin Viaduct**.

The walkway provides the most impressive view of the viaduct, once the longest structure of its kind,

taking the canal which linked Glasgow to the east coast effortlessly across the Kelvin valley. A walk along the quiet canal banks, back into the city, provides a quite different perspective on the city, one of greater ease and tranquillity.

As it follows the route of Maryhill Road, a step away from the canal banks will bring you to **Firhill Stadium**, the home of one of Glasgow's lesser known football clubs Partick Thistle, and **Queen's Cross Church**.

This is Mackintosh's only church building, although it no longer functions as such, but as the headquarters of the Charles Rennie Mackintosh Society. The nearby Ruchill Parish Church Halls, also by Mackintosh, don't command quite the same presence.

The canal completes its route to Glasgow at **Spiers Wharf**, former commercial buildings which are now transformed into smart leisure, business and residential units.

There's one other gem to the north worth exploring. Hidden along an obscure country road at **Robroyston**, set slightly back in a field, is the place thought to be where William Wallace was captured by the English in 1305. A 20-foot high cross marks the spot.

EAST OF GLASGOW CROSS

To take the route east from Glasgow Cross beyond the Barras market and the curiously named **Shipka Pass** (for some strange reason, named after the battle between the Russians and the Turks) is to venture into the Calton district, an area of the city associated with Glasgow's earliest history, though most of the references remain only in street names rather than any extant buildings.

Gallowgate was, as it suggests, the way to the gallows which were situated around Barrack Street. Just off Gallowgate was the famous Saracen's Head, Glasgow's first hotel. Built in 1754 with stones from the ruined Bishop's Castle, it was finally demolished in 1903. The hotel's ancient punchbowl is on view at the People's Palace.

Two of Gallowgate's original crow-stepped tenement buildings have, however, been renovated including the one which houses **Hielan Jessie's** public house, reputedly a regular haunt of Highland soldiers once stationed nearby.

A memorial plaque in the **Calton Burial Ground**, along Abercrombie Street, is a telling reminder of the other side of 18th-century Glasgow, the struggle of the working class. It lists the names of the six Calton Weavers gunned down during the riot which ended the Weaver's strike of 1871.

Eastwards again, and the Parkhead area is famous for two things: **Celtic Park**, the home of Celtic Football Club, which runs guided tours from its new visitor centre; and **Parkhead Forge**, once a major ironworks notorious for the ferocious flames which lit the sky at night, and now replaced by a gleaming glass-roofed modern shopping centre.

Even within this former heavy industrial area, the city fathers still found room to create open spaces. **Tollcross Park**, just east of Parkhead Cross, is justly famous for its rose beds, and provides the venue each year for the Glasgow International Rose Trials.

◄ *Mackintosh designed his only ecclesiastical building, Queen's Cross Church on Maryhill Road, in 1899. No longer operating as a church, it is now the head-quarters of the Charles Rennie Mackintosh Society. As well as being an architectural treasure in its own right, it contains an exhibition area, reference library and specialist shop.*

SOUTH SIDE

The fact that most of the main attractions on the South Side of the River Clyde are spread out across a wider area does not present a problem. The Glasgow underground, which largely serves

today's city centre and the west end, also provides easy access around the area of the south side nearest to the river. Alighting from the underground at Govan will bring you close to the historic **Govan Old Parish Church** which is one of the oldest ecclesiastical sites in Scotland. It dates back to the time of St Constantine who founded the original church in the 6th century. His sarcophagus lies within the chancel and is just one of many ancient relics to be found within these historic church grounds. Among them is a large collection of stones (26 out of almost fifty uncovered in the 19th century), thought originally to have formed a Druidic circle.

Close to Govan is one of Scotland's most famous football grounds, **Ibrox Stadium**, the home of Glasgow Rangers. A measure of the club's success can best be seen in the Trophy Room which is literally crammed with trophies from all over the world, including the coveted European Cup Winners' Cup of 1971.

In nearby **Bellahouston Park**, with its characteristic mound, is one of the most fascinating examples of the work of Charles Rennie Mackintosh, the **House for an Art Lover**. What makes it unique among Mackintosh buildings is that it was only constructed during the early 1990s, based on a design which Mackintosh submitted in 1901 for a competition run by a German magazine.

A tour of the interior highlights the total individuality of Mackintosh, particularly the Dining Room with its vivid decorative details and stylish furniture, and the bright, sun-filled Drawing Room, a curious feature of which is the modern grand piano disguised cleverly within a brilliant white cabinet in Mackintosh style.

A genuine Mackintosh musical design exists across Dumbreck Road in the elegant **Craigie Hall**, once a residential villa, now a business centre. The main building was by his senior colleague, John Honeyman, but Mackintosh was involved in extending the building in the 1890s and in modelling some of the internal fittings, which included a unique organ case.

Closeby, beside Shields Road underground station, Mackintosh's style is once again a feature of **Scotland Street School**. After years of indecision over the building's future once it had ceased to function as a school, it was reopened in 1991 as the popular **Museum of Education**. Classrooms furnished in various period styles offer an excellent insight into school life in Scotland over the past century, all the more remarkable for being set within a building whose architectural details – like the delicate coloured glass motifs which grace the full length staircase windows – are exquisite and unique.

On the western edge of Pollokshields are the

◄ One of the most exciting projects to form part of Glasgow's year as European City of Culture 1990 was the instigation of plans to build a Mackintosh house which existed only in designs and drawings. The House for an Art Lover – Mackintosh's competition entry in 1901 for a German magazine – was finally erected in 1996 in Glasgow's Bellahouston Park, and operates as a visitor attraction, conference venue and as part of Glasgow School of Art's postgraduate school.

extensive grounds of **Pollok Country Park**, once the estate belonging to the Stirling Maxwell family who gifted it, along with their ancestral home, to the city of Glasgow. A favourite jogging circuit, there's always activity going on within the grounds, and plenty to look at, from the long-haired Highland cattle to the fine gardens of **Pollok House**.

Designed by William Adam in the mid 18th century and completed by his son John, Pollok House is one of the most endearing stately homes in Scotland. Relatively modest in scale, it occupies a magnificent south-facing position overlooking the White Cart River and what is now one of Glasgow's exclusive golf courses.

Recently taken over by the National Trust for Scotland, its collection of Spanish and other European paintings, including works by El Greco, Goya and William Blake, is open to the public. Equally fascinating are the house's collections of porcelain, Spanish glass and furniture.

When the new purpose-built gallery for Glasgow's **Burrell Collection** was opened in the centre of Pollok Park in 1983, it drew attention from all around the world, and rightly so. Here is a collection so vast and so varied, and so astonishingly individual, that very little compares with it, other than perhaps that of William Randolph Hearst. It is a gallery you have to visit more than once just to begin to take it all in.

Burrell bequeathed the collection to the city after his death in 1958. His original stipulation, however, was that it should be housed in a gallery no less than 16 miles out of the city in order to escape the polluted atmosphere which Glasgow, at that time, was infamous for. The delay in erecting that gallery turned out to be fortuitous. By the time the go-ahead was finally given, Glasgow's air had become considerably cleaner, Burrell's conditions were contested successfully, and a beautiful new gallery only three

▶ *For many years, Sir William Burrell's priceless collection of paintings, ceramics, tapestries, stained glass, and numerous other curiosities, lay out of sight within the city's museum vaults. In 1983 an award-winning custom-built gallery was opened in the quiet open spaces of Pollok Country Park, built exclusively to house the Burrell Collection.*

miles from the city centre was sanctioned.

Sir William Burrell was one of Glasgow's richest shipowners who, during his long life, collected artefacts of every sort; medieval tapestries and furniture, paintings ranging from Renaissance masters to the Glasgow Boys, porcelain from the Orient and ancient Egypt, church roofs, and one of the finest collections of stained glass in the UK. The gallery, designed by Barry Gasson, places this priceless

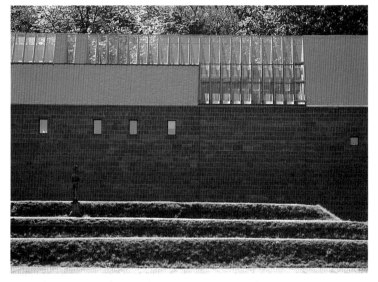

bric-a-brac in a modern and imaginative setting that shows it off at its best.

The only posthumous purchase for the collection – the giant stone Warwick Vase – acts as a powerful symbol of the overall scale of the collection. Themed displays are interspersed with furnished reconstructions of the rooms which Burrell once inhabited himself at his Borders home, Hutton Castle.

Another eye-catching feature is the placement within the structure of authentic castle gateways, purchased by Burrell, including an arched doorway from Hornby Castle in Yorkshire, and even one bought from Randolph Hearst's collection and shipped stone by stone from the United States.

The rich legacies of Glasgow's wealthy entre-
preneurs stretch to the city's limits, and thanks to
the recent commendable investigative efforts of
Historic Scotland and the National Trust for
Scotland, **Holmwood House**, the home of
19th century paper-mill owner James Couper –
towards Cathcart on Netherlee Road – is now
on view to the public (April-October, daily each
afternoon).

Here is the architect Alexander 'Greek' Thomson at his most inventive and most imaginative.
The large mansion house is a highly individual,
almost story-book adaptation of classical Greek
architecture, with heavily ornamented wood, plaster
and marble. What makes it particularly fascinating
is the fact that the restoration process is ongoing,
and part of the visitor experience.

Back towards the city, bordering Pollokshaws
Road is another of the city's major recreational
areas, **Queen's Park**. Laid out in 1862, it is often
thought that the Queen referred to is Victoria. In
fact, the park commemorates a much earlier
Scottish monarch, Mary Queen of Scots, and her

defeat at the Battle of Langside in 1568 which took place on the southern edge of the park. **Battlefield Monument**, a decorative column erected in 1888, marks the spot.

From its highest vantage point – some 209 ft above sea level – Queen's Park offers an unrivalled view of the city and surrounding area. On a clear day, even Ben Lomond is visible.

In nearby Mount Florida is **Hampden Park**, home of Scotland's oldest football team, Queen's Park, and Scotland's national football stadium. Recent development has transformed it into a modern facility, part of which now contains Glasgow's new **Football Museum**, a collection of unique exhibits celebrating Scotland's national sporting game.

Just as the cathedral area has its Necropolis burial ground, so too the **Southern Necropolis** was created within the Gorbals area on the south of the river. Opened in 1840, it did not have the same grand aspirations of its city-centre counterpart, but simply aimed to provide a respectable final resting place for the population of the overcrowded south side.

Over 250,000 lie buried in Glasgow's most densely packed graveyard, among them some notable names like Sir Thomas Lipton and Alexander 'Greek' Thomson. Somewhat ironically, Thomson's grave (sadly neglected for so many years) lies within sight of his Caledonia Street Church, all that remains of which is a disembodied façade.

Along the short route back to the River Clyde, and its passage over towards Glasgow Cross, the **Citizens' Theatre**, noted for its bold and challenging productions, is a poignant reminder that the city has a long and unique cultural heritage which is entrenched in a populace as willing to look outwards as to express its own identity confidently, proudly and nearly always with a smile.

◄ *So much of the unique classical style of Alexander 'Greek' Thomson has been lost through unnecessary demolition over the years. Recent restoration has, however, returned one of his masterpieces to its former glory. Holmwood House, on Glasgow's south side, is a wonderful example of Thomson at his boldest and most imaginative.*

INFORMATION DIRECTORY

Please note: It is advisable to check all opening hours in advance. Information is believed to be correct at the time of publication but names and telephone numbers may be subject to change. When telephoning from Glasgow, omit 0141 from all numbers. Addresses are all Glasgow unless otherwise stated.

ACCOMMODATION
Information & booking service for Hotels & Guest Houses are available through Tourist Information Centres (see page 77).

Caravan & Camping Sites
Craigendmuir Park
Campsie View, Stepps, G33 6AF
Tel: 0141 779 4159
(open March - October)

Strathclyde Park
366 Hamilton Road,
Motherwell, ML1 3ED
Tel: 01698 266155
(open April - October)

Youth Hostels
Glasgow Hostel
7/8 Park Terrace, G3 6BY
Tel: 0141 332 3004

BANKS / BUREAUX DE CHANGE/ POST OFFICE
Banks
Most city banks provide currency exchange facilities. Normal banking hours are 0930 to 1630 Monday-Friday.

Bureaux de Change
Tourist Information Centre
11 George Square,
G2 1DY
Tel: 0141 204 4400

American Express
Lunn Poly
19-21 Gordon Street, G1 3PR
Tel: 0141 204 2324

Thomas Cook
Glasgow Central Station
Tel: 0141 226 5218

Thomas Cook
Glasgow International Airport
Tel: 0141 800 1300

Post Office
Central Post Office
47 St Vincent Street,
G2 5QX
Tel: 0345 223344

CINEMAS
ABC Cinema
326 Sauchiehall Street,
G2 3JB
Tel: 0141 332 1592

ABC Cinema
380 Clarkston Road, G44 3JL
Tel: 0141 633 2123

Glasgow Film Theatre
12 Rose Street, G3 6RB
Tel: 0141 332 6535

Grosvenor Cinema
39-41 Ashton Lane, G12 8SJ
Tel: 0141 339 4298

Odeon Cinema
56 Renfield Street, G2 1NF
Tel: 0141 332 3413

Odeon Cinema
The Quay, Paisley Road,
G5 8NP
Tel: 0141 418 0111

FESTIVALS / EVENTS
Celtic Connections (January)
Glasgow Royal Concert Hall
Tel: 0141 332 6633

Glasgow International
Jazz Festival (July)
Tel: 0141 552 3552

Royal Scottish National
Orchestra Proms (June)
Glasgow Royal Concert Hall
Tel: 0141 332 6633

West End Festival (June)
Tel: 0141 341 0844

World Pipe Band Championships
(August)
Glasgow Green
Tel: 0141 221 5414

LIBRARIES
Mitchell Library
North Street, G3 7DN
Tel: 0141 287 2999

Stirling's Library
62 Miller Street, G1 1DT
Tel: 0141 221 1876

LOST PROPERTY
Glasgow Central Station
Tel: 0141 335 4352

Strathclyde Police
173 Pitt Street, G2 4JS
Tel: 0141 532 2468 / 2609

MEDICAL SERVICES
For minor illness your place
of accommodation will
normally be able to advise
you on a local doctor or
dentist.

Emergencies
Telephone 999 (police,
ambulance & fire brigade)

Hospitals
Glasgow Dental Hospital
378 Sauchiehall Street, G2 3JZ
Tel: 0141 211 9600

Glasgow Royal Infirmary
84-86 Castle Street, G41 4NG
Tel: 0141 211 4000

Southern General Hospital
1345 Govan Road,
G51 4TF
Tel: 0141 201 1100

Victoria Infirmary
Langside Road, G42 9TY
Tel: 0141 201 6000

Western Infirmary
Dumbarton Road, G11 6NT
Tel: 0141 211 2000

**MUSEUMS, ART GALLERIES,
VISITOR ATTRACTIONS**

Art Gallery and Museum,
Kelvingrove
Argyle Street, G3 8AG
Tel: 0141 287 2690

The Burrell Collection
2060 Pollokshaws Road, G43 1AT
Tel: 0141 649 7151

Celtic Football Club Visitor Centre
Celtic Park, G40 3RE
Tel: 0141 551 4308

Centre for Contemporary Arts
350 Sauchiehall Street, G2 3JD
Tel: 0141 332 7521

City Chambers
George Square, G2 1DU
Tel: 0141 287 2000

Clyde Maritime Centre
Yorkhill Quay, G3 8QA
Tel: 0141 339 0631

Gallery of Modern Art
Queen Street, G1 3AZ
Tel: 0141 229 1996

Glasgow Cathedral
Castle Street, G4 0RH
Tel: 0141 552 6891

Glasgow Necropolis
Castle Street, G4 0RH

Glasgow School of Art
167 Renfrew Street, G3 6RQ
Tel: 0141 353 4526

Glasgow Zoo Park
Calder Park, Uddingston, G71 7RZ
Tel: 0141 771 1185

Govan Old Parish Church
Govan Road, G51 3UU
Tel: 0141 445 1941

Holmwood House (NTS)
61-63 Netherlee Road, G44 3YG
Tel: 0141 637 2129

House for an Art Lover
Bellahouston Park, G41 5BW
Tel: 0141 353 4770

Hunterian Art Gallery
University of Glasgow, G12 8QQ
Tel: 0141 330 5431

Hunterian Museum
University of Glasgow, G12 8QQ
Tel: 0141 330 4221

Hutcheson's Hall (NTS)
158 Ingram Street, G1 1EJ
Tel: 0141 552 8391

McLellan Galleries
270 Sauchiehall Street, G2 3EH
Tel: 0141 331 1854

Martyrs' School
Parson Street, G4 0PX
Tel: 0141 946 6600

Museum of Transport
1 Bunhouse Road, G3 8DP
Tel: 0141 287 2720

People's Palace
Glasgow Green, G40 1AT
Tel: 0141 554 0223

Pollok House
2060 Pollokshaws Road, G43 1AT
Tel: 0141 616 6410

Provand's Lordship
3 Castle Street, G4 0RH
Tel: 0141 553 2557

Queen's Cross Church
(Charles Rennie Mackintosh
Society headquarters)
870 Garscube Road, G20 7EL
Tel: 0141 946 6600

St Mungo Heritage Centre
Tennent Caledonian Breweries
161 Duke Street, G31 1JD
Tel: 0141 552 6552,
Ext. 3822

St Mungo Museum
of Religious Life & Art
2 Castle Street, G4 0RH
Tel: 0141 553 2557

Scotland Street School
225 Scotland Street,
G5 8QB
Tel: 0141 429 1202

Sharmanka Kinetic Gallery
& Theatre
109 Trongate, G1 5HD
Tel: 0141 552 7080

Springburn Museum
Atlas Square, Ayr Street,
G21 4BW
Tel: 0141 557 1405

Tenement House
145 Buccleuch Street,
G3 6QN
Tel: 0141 333 0183

Trades Hall of Glasgow
85 Glassford Street, G1 1UH
Tel: 0141 552 2418

University of Glasgow
Visitor Centre
University Avenue, G12 8QQ
Tel: 0141 330 5511

Willow Tea Rooms
217 Sauchiehall Street, G2 3EX
Tel: 0141 332 0521

PLACES OF WORSHIP
Church of Scotland
Glasgow Cathedral
Castle Street, G4 0RH
Tel: 0141 552 6891

Wellington Church
University Avenue, G12 8LE
Tel: 0141 339 0454

Baptist
Adelaide Place Baptist Church
209 Bath Street, G2 4HZ
Tel: 0141 248 4970

Buddhist
Glasgow Buddhist Centre
329 Sauchiehall Street, G2 3HW
Tel: 0141 333 0524

Hindu

The Hindu Mandir
1 La Belle Place, G3 7LH
Tel: 0141 332 0482

Islamic

Central Mosque
1 Mosque Avenue, G5 9TA
Tel: 0141 429 3132

Jewish

Garnethill Synagogue
129 Hill Street, G3 6UG
Tel: 0141 332 4151

Methodist

Partick Methodist Church
524 Dumbarton Road,
G11 6SN
Tel: 0141 339 1409

Roman Catholic

St Aloysius Church
Garnethill, Rose Street,
G3 6RE
Tel: 0141 332 3039

St Andrew's Cathedral
168 Clyde Street, G1 4ER
Tel: 0141 221 3096

Scottish Episcopal

St Mary's Cathedral
Great Western Road,
G4 9JB
Tel: 0141 339 6691

POLICE

Strathclyde Police
St Enoch Centre,
St Enoch Square, G1 4BH
Tel: 0141 532 3278

RESTAURANTS

Glasgow has a rich variety of restaurants, bistros and bars in which you can not only sample quality traditional cuisine made with the best of Scottish produce, but also a truly international range of cooking. The city centre and west end provide the main concentration of good eating spots, particularly Indian, Italian and Chinese restaurants.

SHOPPING

Glasgow is the UK's second largest retail centre outwith London, offering a range of outlets from major high street names to more exclusive designer outlets like Armani and Versace. The main shopping areas are on Argyle Street, Buchanan Street and Sauchiehall Street, right in the city centre. A range of shopping malls includes the individual and chic Princes Square on Buchanan Street, the enormous St Enoch Centre on St Enoch Square, and the new Buchanan Galleries.

Outwith the city centre, the West End offers an intriguing range of art and craft shops. The weekend Barras market to the east of Glasgow Cross is well worth a visit – a unique Glasgow experience!

SPORT & LEISURE
Football Clubs

Celtic Football Club
Celtic Park, G40 3RE
Tel: 0141 556 2611

Partick Thistle Football Club
Firhill Stadium, G20 7BA
Tel: 0141 945 4811

Queen's Park Football Club
Hampden Park, G42 9BA
Tel: 0141 632 1275

Rangers Football Club
Ibrox Stadium, G51 2XD
Tel: 0141 427 8500

Leisure Centres
Kelvin Hall Sports Arena
Argyle Street, G3 8AW
Tel: 0141 357 2525

North Woodside Leisure Centre
Braid Square, G4 9YB
Tel: 0141 332 8102

Scotstoun Leisure Centre
Danes Drive, G14 9HO
Tel: 0141 959 4000

Tollcross Park Leisure Centre
Wellshot Road,
Tollcross, G32 7QR
Tel: 0141 763 2345

Parks & Gardens
Bellahouston Park
Dumbreck Road, G52 1BA
Tel: 0141 427 0558

Botanic Gardens
730 Great Western Road,
G12 0UE
Tel: 0141 334 2422

Glasgow Green
Greendyke Street, G40

Greenbank Garden
Flenders Road, G76 8RB
Clarkston
Tel: 0141 639 3281

Kelvingrove Park
Otago Street, G12 8NR
Tel: 0141 334 6363

Linn Park
Simshill Road, G44 5TA
Tel: 0141 771 6372

Pollok Country Park
Pollokshaws Road, G43 1AT
Tel: 0141 632 9299

Queen's Park
520 Langside Road, G42 9QL
Tel: 0141 632 1327

Victoria Park & Fossil Grove
1 Victoria Park Drive North,
G14 9UY
Tel: 0141 959 9087

THEATRES & CONCERT HALLS
The Citizens' Theatre
119 Gorbals Street, G5 9DS
Tel: 0141 429 5561

City Halls
Candleriggs, G1 1NQ
Tel: 0141 287 5024

Glasgow Royal Concert Hall
2 Sauchiehall Street, G2 3NY
Tel: 0141 332 6633

Henry Wood Hall
73 Claremont Street, G3 7JB
Tel: 0141 204 4540

King's Theatre
294 Bath Street, G2 4JN
Tel: 0141 248 5153

The Mitchell Theatre
3 Granville Street, G3 7DR
Tel: 0141 287 4855

The Royal Scottish Academy
of Music & Drama
100 Renfrew Street, G2 3DB
Tel: 0141 332 4101

Scottish Exhibition &
Conference Centre
Finnieston Street, G3 8YW
Tel: 0141 248 3000

Theatre Royal
Hope Street, G2 3QA
Tel: 0141 332 9000

Tramway Theatre
25 Albert Drive, G41 2PE
Tel: 0141 422 2023

Tron Theatre
63 Trongate, G1 5HB
Tel: 0141 552 4267

**TOURIST INFORMATION
CENTRES**
Greater Glasgow &
Clyde Valley Tourist Board
11 George Square,
G2 1DY
Tel: 0141 204 4400

Glasgow International Airport
(International Arrivals)
Paisley PA3 2ST
Tel: 0141 848 4440

TICKETS & TOURS
Boat Tours
P.S.*Waverley*
Sailings on the Firth of Clyde,
June - August
Tel: 0141 221 8152

Bus Tours
Discovering Glasgow Tours &
Guide Friday tours operate
open-top city bus tours daily
throughout the day. The
main pick-up point is at
George Square.

City Tours
Information & bookings for
most tours available at the
Tourist Information Centre,
George Square.

Day Tripper Ticket
Unlimited travel for one day on
underground, rail & most bus
services around Glasgow.

Roundabout Ticket
Allows unlimited travel by train
& underground for one day.

Underground Heritage Trail
Unlimited travel by underground
for one day, with detailed map
of walks & attractions within
reach of each station.

Walking Tours
The Glasgow Literary Tour
A city walk taking in Glasgow's
literary connections in the
company of professional actors.
Tel: 0800 328 3024

Mercat Tours
Ghost tours of Glasgow departing daily from the Tourist Information Centre, George Square.
Tel: 0141 772 0022

Scottish Tourist Guides Association
Guided walks of the city centre.
Tel: 0870 6073071

Taxi Tours
Glasgow Wide TOA Ltd
1- to 3-hour tours of Glasgow, including *Glasgow by Night* tour.
Tel: 0141 332 6666 / 7070

TRAVEL
Air
Glasgow International Airport
Tel: 0141 887 1111
Shuttle buses operate between the airport & Glasgow city centre (8 miles).

Bus
Buchanan Bus Station
Killermont Street,
G2 3NP
Tel: 0141 332 7133

Rail
Glasgow Central Station
(for services to the south & west)
Tel: 0345 484950 (24 hours)

Glasgow Queen Street Station
(for services to the north & east)
Tel: 0345 484950 (24 hours)

Taxi
Airport Taxi Service
Tel: 0141 848 4900

Glasgow Wide TOA Ltd
Tel: 0141 332 6666 / 7070

Paisley & Glasgow Airport Taxi
Tel: 0141 887 8811

The Travel Centre
St Enoch Square, G1 4BW
Tel: 0141 226 4826
Tickets for local transport, zone-cards, coach tours & excursions.

Underground
Covering parts of city centre, west end & south side.
Tel: 0141 226 4826

BOOK LIST

Berry & White, *Glasgow Observed*, 1981.
Buchanan, William (ed.), *Mackintosh's Masterwork – The Glasgow School of Art*, 1989.
Daiches, David, *Glasgow*, 1982.
Fisher, Joe, *The Glasgow Encyclopedia*, 1994.
Foreman, Carol, *Street Names of the City of Glasgow*, 1997.
Gibb, Andrew, *The Making of a City*, 1983.
McKean, Walker & Walker, *Central Glasgow – An Illustrated Guide*, 1993.
Massie, Allan, *Glasgow: Portraits of a City*, 1989.
Munro, M, *The Patter*,1985.
Smart, Aileen, *Villages of Glasgow*, (Vols 1&2), 1989.
Walker, F M, *Song of the Clyde: A History of Clyde Shipbuilding*, 1984.
Wordsall, Frank, *Victorian City*, 1982.

Index